Magic Mandalas 2

colouring book for kids

L.J. Knight

This book features fifty original abstract mandala illustrations. These mandalas are designed especially for children, who can gain the same calming benefits and enjoyment from colouring mandalas as adults. This is also a great book for anyone who likes to colour simple designs.

These images can be coloured with pencils, markers and other media. If you're using markers, or you tend to press heavily on the page, it's helpful to place a sheet of card or scrap paper under the page you're colouring to protect the image underneath. There is a blank page at the end of the book that can be removed and used for this purpose.

This title was originally published in October 2017 as *Magic Mandalas 2 Colouring Book For Kids* by Tigerlynx.

Second Edition published in July 2018.

#1

#3

#4

#5

#6

#8

#10

#15

© L.J. Knight

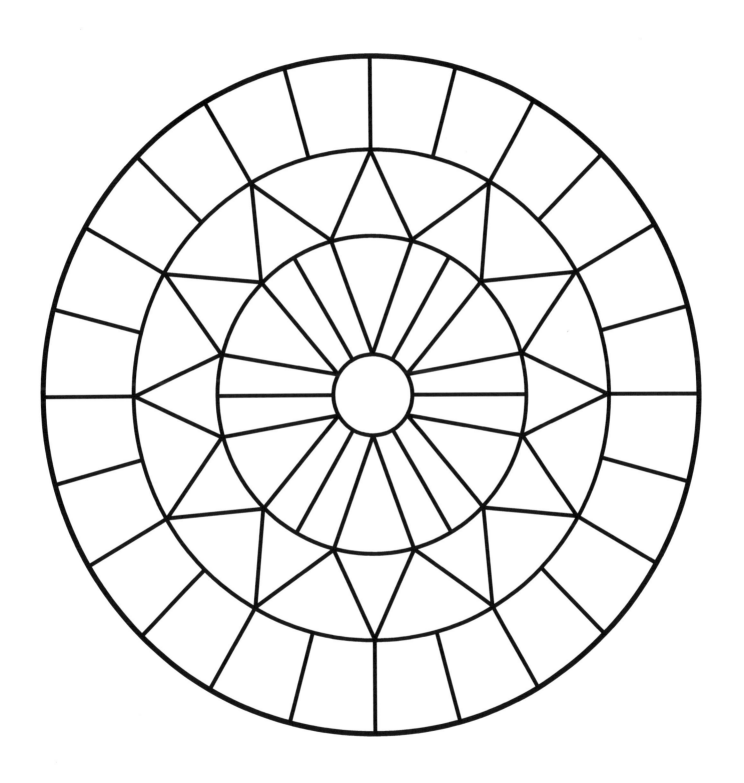

#19

#23

#24

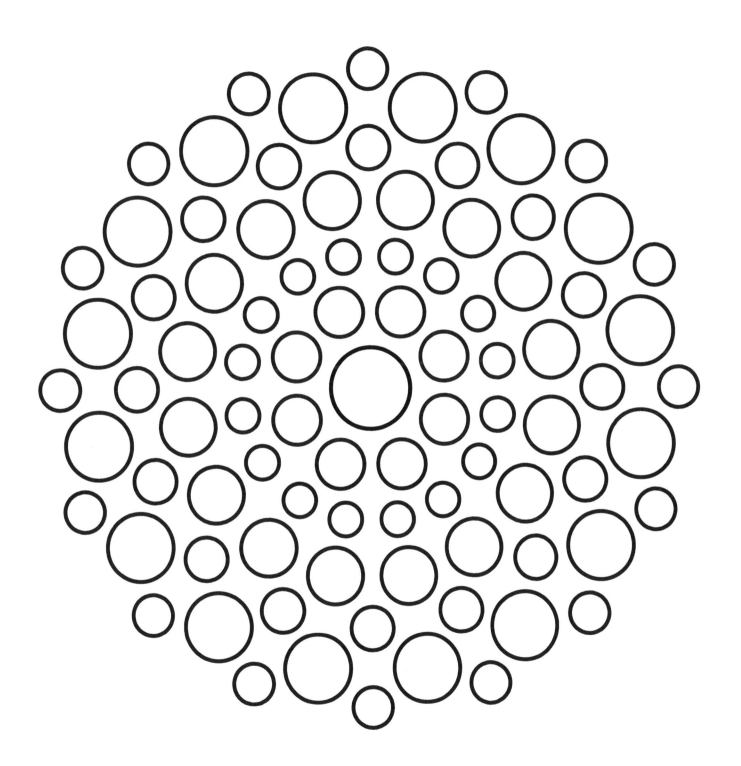

#26

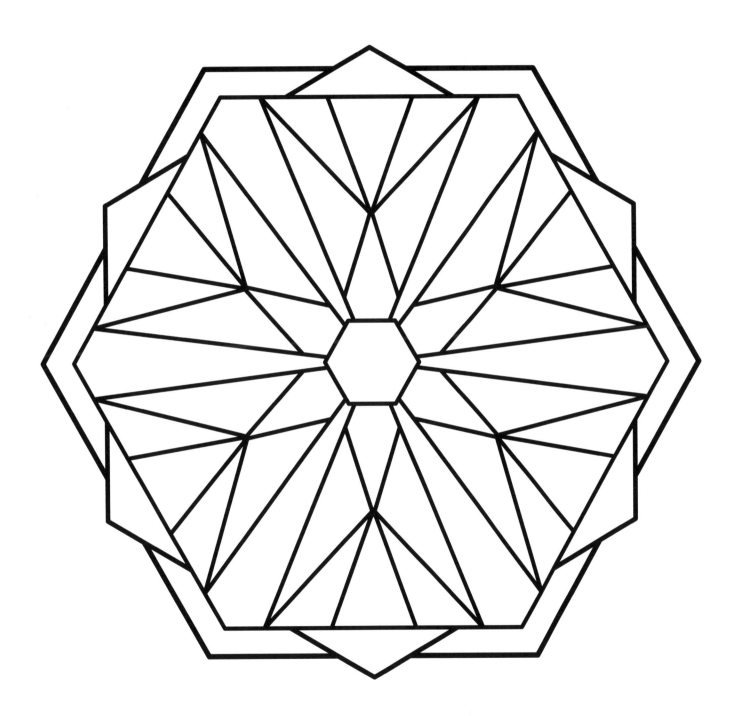

#33

#33

#42

Bonus
Pages

The following pages contain free sample designs
from some of my other colouring books

For more information, visit
ljknightart.com/colouring

Easy Mandalas Colouring Book
ljknightart.com/colouring/easy-mandalas

Through the Kaleidoscope Colouring Book - ljknightart.com/colouring/kaleidoscope

Magic Mandalas Colouring Book For Kids
ljknightart.com/colouring/magic-mandalas

Extra Easy Flower Mandalas Colouring Book For Kids
ljknightart.com/colouring/easy-flower-mandalas

Thank you for buying *Magic Mandalas 2*. I have a growing range of colouring books with various themes, which are available from Amazon and other retailers. For more information, visit my website at **ljknightart.com/colouring**

This page has intentionally been left blank, so you can remove it and place it under the page you're colouring to protect the image underneath, or use it for colour testing.

Made in the USA
Middletown, DE
25 June 2022

67751275R00068